Jossey-Bass Teacher

Jossey-Bass Teacher provides K–12 teachers with essential knowledge and tools to create a positive and lifelong impact on student learning. Trusted and experienced educational mentors offer practical classroom-tested and theory-based teaching resources for improving teaching practice in a broad range of grade levels and subject areas. From one educator to another, we want to be your first source to make every day your best day in teaching. *Jossey-Bass Teacher* resources serve two types of informational needs—essential knowledge and essential tools.

Essential knowledge resources provide the foundation, strategies, and methods from which teachers may design curriculum and instruction to challenge and excite their students. Connecting theory to practice, essential knowledge books rely on a solid research base and time-tested methods, offering the best ideas and guidance from many of the most experienced and well-respected experts in the field.

Essential tools save teachers time and effort by offering proven, ready-to-use materials for in-class use. Our publications include activities, assessments, exercises, instruments, games, ready reference, and more. They enhance an entire course of study, a weekly lesson, or a daily plan. These essential tools provide insightful, practical, and comprehensive materials on topics that matter most to K–12 teachers.

Fantasy Football and Mathematics

Student Name: _____

Fantasy Sports and Mathematics Series

Fantasy Football and Mathematics

Student Workbook

Dan Flockhart

BICENTENNIAL
1807
WILEY
2007
BICENTENNIAL

JB JOSSEY-BASS

Published by Jossey-Bass
A Wiley Imprint
989 Market Street, San Francisco, CA 94103-1741   www.josseybass.com

Jossey-Bass books and products are available through most bookstores. To contact Jossey-Bass directly call our Customer Care Department within the U.S. at 800-956-7739, outside the U.S. at 317-572-3986, or fax 317-572-4002.

Jossey-Bass also publishes its books in a variety of electronic formats. Some content that appears in print may not be available in electronic books.

ISBN: 0-978-7879-9448-8

Printed in the United States of America
FIRST EDITION
PB Printing   10 9 8 7 6 5 4 3 2 1

About the Author

Dan Flockhart received his multiple-subject teaching credential from California State University, East Bay in 1988. He taught mathematics in grades 5 through 8 for eleven years at St. Matthew's Episcopal Day School in San Mateo, California, where he incorporated fantasy sports into his math curriculum. He has also taught general studies classes at College of the Redwoods in Eureka, California. He received a master of arts degree in education from Humboldt State University in 2005; the title of his thesis was "Teacher Perceptions of the Effects of Fantasy Football in the Teaching of Mathematics." Flockhart has enjoyed participating in fantasy sports for over twenty-five years.

In addition to authoring the Fantasy Sports and Mathematics series, Flockhart maintains a Web site, www.fantasysportsmath.com, where teachers can participate in forums and contests and find out more about the series.

To my former students at
St. Matthew's Episcopal Day School

Acknowledgments

This book would not have been possible without the help and support of several people. I thank Sara, Ann, and Cathy for their valuable input. I am also thankful to Kate, who made all of this possible. You are one of my angels! I was also lucky to work with wonderful production editors, Elizabeth and Susan, and copyeditors, Carolyn and Bev. They were fun to work with and I was impressed with their willingness to do whatever it took to produce the best possible product. My thanks go out as well to Chris for creating one of the best covers I've ever seen. In addition, I'm grateful to Lena for ensuring that all the math is accurate and Tiffany for her continual support as well as the countless hours she spent on this project. Finally, I express my gratitude to Tom, who introduced me to the game, and John, the master of the cheat sheet.

Contents

Graphing Activities

Graphing

Practice Worksheets

Assessment   121

Fantasy Football and Mathematics Handouts

Description and Rules

Fantasy Football and Mathematics is a game in which you create and manage a team of players from professional, college, or high school football teams (high school players can select themselves!). Players earn points by scoring touchdowns and two-point conversions and accumulating passing, rushing, and receiving yards. Players lose points for interceptions thrown and fumbles lost. Each week you will find the sum of the points earned by your players. The goal of the game is to accumulate the highest number of points.

How to Select Players

There are two options for selecting players. Your teacher will decide which option your class will be using.

Option 1. You have a salary cap of $40 million to select eleven professional players and two team defenses. Your instructor will provide you with a list of players and their costs. Table 1 lists the number of players selected at each position, as well as the number of players in a starting lineup.

You may select the same players or defensive teams as other students. For example, several students may want to select the same quarterback, which is fine.

Option 2. Each week you select one team. For example, if you live in Atlanta, you may decide to select your hometown team for the first week of the game. However, you may not choose that team in later weeks, because you can select each team only once during the game. Unlike in option 1, you will compute points using team statistics rather than from individual statistics. For example, if your team had a total of 127 yards rushing, you would use that number to compute points.

Table 1.   Complete Roster and Starting Lineup Each Week

Position	Number of Players Selected for Each Position	Number of Players Selected for Starting Lineup
Quarterback	2	1
Running back	3	2
Wide receiver (includes tight ends)	4	3
Kicker	2	1
Team defense	2	1

Description and Rules *(Cont'd.)*

It is important for you to select high-scoring teams that are playing against weak opponents in order to maximize the points you will earn. That said, there is as much luck in Fantasy Football as there is skill.

If you use option 1 to select players, your rosters will remain the same for the duration of the game (with the exception of trades, which are explained in the next section). If you use option 2, your players will change every week.

Trades

You may trade players if you selected players using option 1. Trades do not have to be position for position. For example, you might decide to trade a kicker for a quarterback. But in that case, you would have only one kicker. If that kicker got injured, you would not have a kicker in your starting lineup, which is not advised. If you are thinking about making a trade, you need to consider its impact on your full roster. If you do make a trade, it is important that you make the necessary changes to your Fantasy team roster.

Salary cap numbers do not apply to trades.

Injuries and Bye Weeks

If you cannot locate a player's name in the box scores, he is probably injured or the team didn't play that week (this is called a *bye week*). *If this occurs, the players' score is counted as zero.* A player who is placed on injured reserve (IR) will not play for the remainder of the season. If a player is declared out for the year and you used option 1 to select players, you may use the portion of the salary cap you spent on that player to purchase another player. A list of injured players can be found in newspapers as well as online at www.fantasysportsmath.com or other sports Web sites.

Fantasy Team Roster

Name of Fantasy Team: _____   Team Owner: _____

Position	Name	Team	Cost
Quarterback			
Quarterback			
Running back			
Running back			
Running back			
Wide receiver			
Wide receiver			
Wide receiver			
Wide receiver			
Kicker			
Kicker			
Team defense			
Team defense			

How to Read Box Scores

Two sections of a fabricated box score are shown below. Box scores are written in several formats. The sections of box scores you will use are usually titled "Scoring Summary" and "Player (or Individual) Statistics." A player (other than a kicker) whose name is listed in the scoring summary has scored a touchdown or passed for a touchdown. (The only exception is a two-point conversion, which occurs when a team elects to try for two points rather than kick the point after a touchdown. On a two-point conversion, a team gets one chance to get the ball in the end zone from the two-yard line.) For example, in Table 1, the first score of the game was a three-yard touchdown run by Aaron Dunlap. Additional touchdowns were scored in the second quarter by Frank Loery, Devan Shalter, Gary Hollings, and Ollie Mays. In addition, Steve Blake and Jesse Wade passed for touchdowns in the second quarter.

Kickers earn points for field goals (FG) and the point after touchdown (PAT). Notice, for example, that Angel Ramos kicked the point after touchdown after the first touchdown of the game. He also kicked a field goal in the first quarter.

Table 1. Sample Box Score: Panthers at Tigers

1ST QUARTER

TD   Aaron Dunlap, 3 Yd run (Angel Ramos kick is good), 9:59. Drive: 9 plays, 63 yards in 5:01.

FG   Angel Ramos 38 Yd, 2:00. Drive: 8 plays, 76 yards in 4:31.

2ND QUARTER

TD   Frank Loery, 8 Yd pass from Steve Blake (Angel Ramos kick is good), 13:43. Drive: 6 plays, 27 yards in 3:08.

TD   Devan Shalter, 40 Yd interception return (Henry Darris 2 Pt. Conversion pass to failed), 4:41.

TD   Gary Hollings, 96 Yd kick return (Angel Ramos kick is good), 4:27.

TD   Ollie Mays, 7 Yd pass from Jesse Wade (Brian Martinez kick is good), 1:14. Drive: 5 plays, 50 yards in 1:26.

3RD QUARTER

FG   Brian Martinez 44 Yd, 12:14. Drive: 8 plays, 26 yards in 2:46.

TD   Mack Knightly, 3 Yd pass from Jesse Wade (Jesse Wade pass to Ty Johnson for 2 Pt. Conversion), 1:54. Drive: 4 plays, 60 yards in 1:41.

4TH QUARTER

FG   Brian Martinez 37 Yd, 11:38. Drive: 9 plays, 71 yards in 3:49.

TD   D.J. Tucker, 1 Yd pass from Jesse Wade (Brian Martinez kick is good), 8:57. Drive: 6 plays, 25 yards in 2:33.

FG   Brian Martinez 26 Yd, 3:22. Drive: 9 plays, 33 yards in 3:48.

TD   Gary Hollings, 15 Yd pass from Steve Blake (Angel Ramos kick is good), 1:24. Drive: 8 plays, 75 yards in 1:58.

Note: TD = touchdown. FG = field goal.

Fantasy Football and Mathematics handouts

How to Read Box Scores *(Cont'd.)*

The touchdowns scored by Devan Shalter and Gary Hollings were scored by players on defensive teams. Therefore, students who had the Panthers or Tigers as their defensive team would earn points. Defensive touchdowns are preceded by phrases such as "interception return," "fumble return," "punt return," "kickoff return," or "fumble recovery in end zone." Defensive teams also earn points by safeties, which occur when an offensive player is tackled in his own end zone. Safeties are listed as such and are rare; there were not any safeties in this game.

Players lose points for interceptions thrown and fumbles lost. The box score in Table 2 shows that Jesse Wade threw one interception (INT), and Gary Hollings and Josh Maris each lost one fumble (FUM).

The starting lineup in Table 3 on page 33 is used for reference purposes throughout this book.

Table 2. Box Score: Panthers at Tigers (Week 1)

PASSING—Panthers				
	CP/AT	YDS	TD	INT
J. Wade	33/48	369	3	1
PASSING—Tigers				
	CP/AT	YDS	TD	INT
S. Blake	19/30	221	2	2
RUSHING—Panthers				
	ATT	YDS	TD	LG
T. Johnson	9	15	0	7
L. Jones	4	14	0	8
J. Wade	4	−1	0	2
RUSHING—Tigers				
	ATT	YDS	TD	LG
A. Dunlap	18	84	1	16
J. Maris	7	34	0	21
Y. Ussif	1	23	0	23
S. Blake	1	3	0	3

(Cont'd.)

How to Read Box Scores *(Cont'd.)*

Table 2.   Box Score: Panthers at Tigers (Week 1) *(Cont'd)*

RECEIVING—Panthers

	REC	YDS	TD	LG
O. Mays	11	171	1	30
D. J. Tucker	9	67	1	19
T. Johnson	6	33	0	11
Mack Knightly	7	98	1	31

RECEIVING—Tigers

	REC	YDS	TD	LG
F. Loery	7	109	1	49
G. Hollings	4	45	1	22
M. Sallinger	1	38	0	38
Y. Ussif	5	24	0	10
T. Faumuina	2	5	0	4

FUMBLES—Panthers

	FUM	LOST	REC	YDS
C. Vickman	1	1	0	0

FUMBLES—Tigers

	FUM	LOST	REC	YDS
G. Hollings	1	1	0	0
J. Maris	1	1	0	0

KICKING—Panthers

	FG	LG	XP	PTS
B. Martinez	3/4	44	2/2	11

KICKING—Tigers

	FG	LG	XP	PTS
A. Ramos	1/1	38	4/4	7

Note: cp = number of completed passes; at = number of passes attempted; yds = number of yards gained; td = number of touchdowns; int = number of interceptions; att = number of rushing attempts; lg = longest(gain); rec = number of receptions; fum = number of fumbles; lost = number of fumbles lost; rec = number of fumbles recovered; fg = field goal; lg = longest(field goal); xp = number of extra points(or PATs); pts = number of points scored

Fantasy Football and Mathematics handouts

How to Read Box Scores *(Cont'd.)*

Table 3. Starting Lineup for the Wildcats

Jesse Wade	Quarterback
Ty Johnson	Running back
Josh Maris	Running back
Ollie Mays	Wide receiver
D. J. Tucker	Wide receiver
Tao Faumuina	Wide receiver
Angel Ramos	Kicker
Tigers	Defense

How to Collect Data

Each week, you will use newspapers or online resources to collect data from one game in which each of your players in your starting lineup participated. Accessing data online is the quickest and easiest method. Statistics are also archived online so you can collect data in case you miss a week or two.

Follow these steps to locate statistics online at www.fantasysportsmath.com:

1. Click the "Get Football Stats" link.
2. On the following page, use the calendar to select the week you are looking for.
3. Find a team that one of your players participated in and click on the box score for that game.

How to Compute Points: Default Scoring System

The default scoring system can be used each week to determine the ranking of students' teams in the game. The default scoring system was designed so that you can plot the weekly points earned for your players to precise numerical values on stacked-bar and multiple-line graphs. This is explained later. However, your teacher may choose a different scoring system.

The points that you earn can be computed by two different methods. One method uses algebra, and the other does not.

The non-algebraic method lists touchdowns, two-point conversions, and yards gained for each player. Points are earned for each set of 25 yards gained from passing, as well as each set of 10 yards gained from rushing or receiving. Consequently, yards gained from passing are divided by 25, and yards gained from rushing or receiving are divided by 10. Quotients are always rounded down to the nearest whole number. For example, Jesse Wade passed for 369 yards, which is divided by 25. The quotient of 14.76 is rounded down to 14. Since there are 14 25s in 369, and each 25 yards is worth $\frac{1}{48}$, 14 is multiplied by $\frac{1}{48}$ to arrive at $\frac{14}{48}$. If students cannot multiply fractions, they can use repeated addition to compute points. This process is also used to compute points earned from rushing and receiving yards, with the exception that you compute the number of 10s rather than the number of 25s.

Table 1 uses the non-algebraic method to compute the points for the Wildcats. The points earned have been computed for the first player (Wade). Your task is to complete this worksheet. Compute points for players from the Panthers–Tigers box score in Handout 3.

The second method of computing points uses algebra; it uses equations that contain variables. These equations are known as *total points equations* because they are used to compute the total points for one week for all players, with the exception of kickers and team defenses.

How to Compute Points:
Default Scoring System *(Cont'd.)*

For Each:	Players Earn:
Kickers	
Point after touchdown (PAT)	$\frac{1}{48}$ or .021
Field goal (FG)	$\frac{1}{16}$ or .063
Quarterbacks, running backs, wide receivers, defenses	
Touchdown (by passing, rushing, or receiving)	$\frac{1}{8}$ or .125
Two point conversion	$\frac{1}{24}$ or .042
Touchdown by a defense	$\frac{1}{8}$ or .125
Safety by a defense	$\frac{1}{24}$ or .042
Interception	$-\frac{1}{12}$ or −.083
Fumble	$-\frac{1}{16}$ or −.063
Passing yards	$\frac{1}{48}$ for every 25 yards
Rushing or receiving yards	$\frac{1}{48}$ for every 10 yards

Note: Decimals are rounded to the nearest thousandth.

Fantasy Football and Mathematics handouts

HANDOUT 6

Practice in Computing Points Using the Default Scoring System

Use the following chart to compute points for the players listed in the Panthers-Tigers box score.

	Wade	Johnson	Maris	Mays	Tucker	Faumuina	Ramos	Tigers
Number of TDs $\times \frac{1}{8}$	$\frac{3}{8}$							
Number of 2-point conversions or safeties $\times \frac{1}{24}$	$\frac{1}{24}$							
Number of passing yards (in 25s) $\times \frac{1}{48}$	$\frac{14}{48}$							
Number of rushing yards (in 10s) $\times \frac{1}{48}$	0							
Number of receiving yards (in 10s) $\times \frac{1}{48}$	0							
Number of PATs $\times \frac{1}{48}$	0							
Number of FGs $\times \frac{1}{16}$	0							
Number of interceptions $\times \left(-\frac{1}{12} \right)$	$-\frac{1}{12}$							
Number of fumbles lost $\times \left(-\frac{1}{16} \right)$	0							
Total individual points:	$\frac{30}{48}$							
Total team points:	$\frac{30}{48} +$							

Copyright © 2007 by Dan Flockhart

Fantasy Football and Mathematics handouts

Default Total Points Equation

In this equation, which is used for quarterbacks, running backs, and wide receivers, the numerical values are the same as the default scoring system:

$$\frac{1}{8}(T) + \frac{1}{24}(V) + \frac{1}{48}(P + R + C) - \frac{1}{12}(I) - \frac{1}{16}(F) = W$$

T = number of touchdowns scored by passing, rushing, or receiving
V = number of two-point conversions scored by passing, rushing, or receiving
P = number of passing yards divided by 25, then rounded down to the nearest whole number
R = number of rushing yards divided by 10, then rounded down to the nearest whole number
C = number of receiving yards divided by 10, then rounded down to the nearest whole number
I = number of interceptions thrown
F = number of fumbles lost
W = total points scored for one week for one individual player

Fantasy Football and Mathematics handouts

Practice in Computing Points Using the Default Total Points Equation

$$\frac{1}{8}\,(T) + \frac{1}{24}\,(V) + \frac{1}{48}\,(P + R + C) - \frac{1}{12}\,(I) - \frac{1}{16}\,(F) = W$$

Use Handout 3 to fill out the following table.

Player	Computation	Points
Wade	$\frac{1}{8}\,(3) + \frac{1}{24}\,(1) + \frac{1}{48}\,(14 + 0 + 0) - \frac{1}{12}\,(1) - \frac{1}{16}\,(0) = W$	
Johnson		
Maris		
Mays		
Tucker		
Faumuina		

HANDOUT 9

Weekly Scoring Worksheet (Week 1)

Fill in the numerical values for scoring criteria in the left column. If you are using the default scoring system, the numerical values are listed on Handout 5. If you are using a different scoring system, your teacher will tell you the numerical values. You can get the statistics you need to fill out this handout at www.fantasysportsmath.com.

	QB	RB 1	RB 2	WR 1	WR 2	WR 3	K	Def
Number of TDs × _____								
Number of two-point conversions or safeties × _____								
Number of passing yards (in 25s) × _____								
Number of rushing yards (in 10s) × _____								
Number of receiving yards (in 10s) × _____								
Number of PATs × _____								
Number of FGs × _____								
Number of interceptions × _____								
Number of fumbles lost × _____								
Total individual points								
Total points for the week:								

Weekly Scoring Worksheet (Week 2)

Fill in the numerical values for scoring criteria in the left column. If you are using the default scoring system, the numerical values are listed on Handout 5. If you are using a different scoring system, your teacher will tell you the numerical values. You can get the statistics you need to fill out this handout at www.fantasysportsmath.com.

	QB	RB 1	RB 2	WR 1	WR 2	WR 3	K	Def
Number of TDs × _____								
Number of two-point conversions or safeties × _____								
Number of passing yards (in 25s) × _____								
Number of rushing yards (in 10s) × _____								
Number of receiving yards (in 10s) × _____								
Number of PATs × _____								
Number of FGs × _____								
Number of interceptions × _____								
Number of fumbles lost × _____								
Total individual points								
Total points for the week:								

Weekly Scoring Worksheet (Week 3)

Fill in the numerical values for scoring criteria in the left column. If you are using the default scoring system, the numerical values are listed on Handout 5. If you are using a different scoring system, your teacher will tell you the numerical values. You can get the statistics you need to fill out this handout at www.fantasysportsmath.com.

	QB	RB 1	RB 2	WR 1	WR 2	WR 3	K	Def
Number of TDs × _____								
Number of two-point conversions or safeties × _____								
Number of passing yards (in 25s) × _____								
Number of rushing yards (in 10s) × _____								
Number of receiving yards (in 10s) × _____								
Number of PATs × _____								
Number of FGs × _____								
Number of interceptions × _____								
Number of fumbles lost × _____								
Total individual points								
Total points for the week:								

Weekly Scoring Worksheet (Week 4)

Fill in the numerical values for scoring criteria in the left column. If you are using the default scoring system, the numerical values are listed on Handout 5. If you are using a different scoring system, your teacher will tell you the numerical values. You can get the statistics you need to fill out this handout at www.fantasysportsmath.com.

	QB	RB 1	RB 2	WR 1	WR 2	WR 3	K	Def
Number of TDs × _____								
Number of two-point conversions or safeties × _____								
Number of passing yards (in 25s) × _____								
Number of rushing yards (in 10s) × _____								
Number of receiving yards (in 10s) × _____								
Number of PATs × _____								
Number of FGs × _____								
Number of interceptions × _____								
Number of fumbles lost × _____								
Total individual points								
Total points for the week:								

Weekly Scoring Worksheet (Week 5)

Fill in the numerical values for scoring criteria in the left column. If you are using the default scoring system, the numerical values are listed on Handout 5. If you are using a different scoring system, your teacher will tell you the numerical values. You can get the statistics you need to fill out this handout at www.fantasysportsmath.com.

	QB	RB 1	RB 2	WR 1	WR 2	WR 3	K	Def
Number of TDs × _____								
Number of two-point conversions or safeties × _____								
Number of passing yards (in 25s) × _____								
Number of rushing yards (in 10s) × _____								
Number of receiving yards (in 10s) × _____								
Number of PATs × _____								
Number of FGs × _____								
Number of interceptions × _____								
Number of fumbles lost × _____								
Total individual points								
Total points for the week:								

Weekly Scoring Worksheet (Week 6)

Fill in the numerical values for scoring criteria in the left column. If you are using the default scoring system, the numerical values are listed on Handout 5. If you are using a different scoring system, your teacher will tell you the numerical values. You can get the statistics you need to fill out this handout at www.fantasysportsmath.com.

	QB	RB 1	RB 2	WR 1	WR 2	WR 3	K	Def
Number of TDs × _____								
Number of two-point conversions or safeties × _____								
Number of passing yards (in 25s) × _____								
Number of rushing yards (in 10s) × _____								
Number of receiving yards (in 10s) × _____								
Number of PATs × _____								
Number of FGs × _____								
Number of interceptions × _____								
Number of fumbles lost × _____								
Total individual points								
Total points for the week:								

Weekly Scoring Worksheet (Week 7)

Fill in the numerical values for scoring criteria in the left column. If you are using the default scoring system, the numerical values are listed on Handout 5. If you are using a different scoring system, your teacher will tell you the numerical values. You can get the statistics you need to fill out this handout at www.fantasysportsmath.com.

	QB	RB 1	RB 2	WR 1	WR 2	WR 3	K	Def
Number of TDs × _____								
Number of two-point conversions or safeties × _____								
Number of passing yards (in 25s) × _____								
Number of rushing yards (in 10s) × _____								
Number of receiving yards (in 10s) × _____								
Number of PATs × _____								
Number of FGs × _____								
Number of interceptions × _____								
Number of fumbles lost × _____								
Total individual points								
Total points for the week:								

Fantasy Football and Mathematics handouts

Weekly Scoring Worksheet (Week 8)

Fill in the numerical values for scoring criteria in the left column. If you are using the default scoring system, the numerical values are listed on Handout 5. If you are using a different scoring system, your teacher will tell you the numerical values. You can get the statistics you need to fill out this handout at www.fantasysportsmath.com.

	QB	RB 1	RB 2	WR 1	WR 2	WR 3	K	Def
Number of TDs × _____								
Number of two-point conversions or safeties × _____								
Number of passing yards (in 25s) × _____								
Number of rushing yards (in 10s) × _____								
Number of receiving yards (in 10s) × _____								
Number of PATs × _____								
Number of FGs × _____								
Number of interceptions × _____								
Number of fumbles lost × _____								
Total individual points								
Total points for the week:								

Weekly Scoring Worksheet (Week 9)

Fill in the numerical values for scoring criteria in the left column. If you are using the default scoring system, the numerical values are listed on Handout 5. If you are using a different scoring system, your teacher will tell you the numerical values. You can get the statistics you need to fill out this handout at www.fantasysportsmath.com.

	QB	RB 1	RB 2	WR 1	WR 2	WR 3	K	Def
Number of TDs × _____								
Number of two-point conversions or safeties × _____								
Number of passing yards (in 25s) × _____								
Number of rushing yards (in 10s) × _____								
Number of receiving yards (in 10s) × _____								
Number of PATs × _____								
Number of FGs × _____								
Number of interceptions × _____								
Number of fumbles lost × _____								
Total individual points								
Total points for the week:								

Weekly Scoring Worksheet (Week 10)

Fill in the numerical values for scoring criteria in the left column. If you are using the default scoring system, the numerical values are listed on Handout 5. If you are using a different scoring system, your teacher will tell you the numerical values. You can get the statistics you need to fill out this handout at www.fantasysportsmath.com.

	QB	RB 1	RB 2	WR 1	WR 2	WR 3	K	Def
Number of TDs × _____								
Number of two-point conversions or safeties × _____								
Number of passing yards (in 25s) × _____								
Number of rushing yards (in 10s) × _____								
Number of receiving yards (in 10s) × _____								
Number of PATs × _____								
Number of FGs × _____								
Number of interceptions × _____								
Number of fumbles lost × _____								
Total individual points								
Total points for the week:								

Peer Signature: _____

Weekly Scoring Worksheet (Week 11)

Fill in the numerical values for scoring criteria in the left column. If you are using the default scoring system, the numerical values are listed on Handout 5. If you are using a different scoring system, your teacher will tell you the numerical values. You can get the statistics you need to fill out this handout at www.fantasysportsmath.com.

	QB	RB 1	RB 2	WR 1	WR 2	WR 3	K	Def
Number of TDs × _____								
Number of two-point conversions or safeties × _____								
Number of passing yards (in 25s) × _____								
Number of rushing yards (in 10s) × _____								
Number of receiving yards (in 10s) × _____								
Number of PATs × _____								
Number of FGs × _____								
Number of interceptions × _____								
Number of fumbles lost × _____								
Total individual points								
Total points for the week:								

Weekly Scoring Worksheet (Week 12)

Fill in the numerical values for scoring criteria in the left column. If you are using the default scoring system, the numerical values are listed on Handout 5. If you are using a different scoring system, your teacher will tell you the numerical values. You can get the statistics you need to fill out this handout at www.fantasysportsmath.com.

	QB	RB 1	RB 2	WR 1	WR 2	WR 3	K	Def
Number of TDs × _____								
Number of two-point conversions or safeties × _____								
Number of passing yards (in 25s) × _____								
Number of rushing yards (in 10s) × _____								
Number of receiving yards (in 10s) × _____								
Number of PATs × _____								
Number of FGs × _____								
Number of interceptions × _____								
Number of fumbles lost × _____								
Total individual points								
Total points for the week:								

Weekly Scoring Worksheet (Week 13)

Fill in the numerical values for scoring criteria in the left column. If you are using the default scoring system, the numerical values are listed on Handout 5. If you are using a different scoring system, your teacher will tell you the numerical values. You can get the statistics you need to fill out this handout at www.fantasysportsmath.com.

	QB	RB 1	RB 2	WR 1	WR 2	WR 3	K	Def
Number of TDs × _____								
Number of two-point conversions or safeties × _____								
Number of passing yards (in 25s) × _____								
Number of rushing yards (in 10s) × _____								
Number of receiving yards (in 10s) × _____								
Number of PATs × _____								
Number of FGs × _____								
Number of interceptions × _____								
Number of fumbles lost × _____								
Total individual points								
Total points for the week:								

Fantasy Football and Mathematics handouts

Weekly Scoring Worksheet (Week 14)

Fill in the numerical values for scoring criteria in the left column. If you are using the default scoring system, the numerical values are listed on Handout 5. If you are using a different scoring system, your teacher will tell you the numerical values. You can get the statistics you need to fill out this handout at www.fantasysportsmath.com.

	QB	RB 1	RB 2	WR 1	WR 2	WR 3	K	Def
Number of TDs × _____								
Number of two-point conversions or safeties × _____								
Number of passing yards (in 25s) × _____								
Number of rushing yards (in 10s) × _____								
Number of receiving yards (in 10s) × _____								
Number of PATs × _____								
Number of FGs × _____								
Number of interceptions × _____								
Number of fumbles lost × _____								
Total individual points								
Total points for the week:								

Peer Signature: _____

Weekly Scoring Worksheet (Week 15)

Fill in the numerical values for scoring criteria in the left column. If you are using the default scoring system, the numerical values are listed on Handout 5. If you are using a different scoring system, your teacher will tell you the numerical values. You can get the statistics you need to fill out this handout at www.fantasysportsmath.com.

	QB	RB 1	RB 2	WR 1	WR 2	WR 3	K	Def
Number of TDs × _____								
Number of two-point conversions or safeties × _____								
Number of passing yards (in 25s) × _____								
Number of rushing yards (in 10s) × _____								
Number of receiving yards (in 10s) × _____								
Number of PATs × _____								
Number of FGs × _____								
Number of interceptions × _____								
Number of fumbles lost × _____								
Total individual points								
Total points for the week:								

Fantasy Football and Mathematics handouts

Weekly Scoring Worksheet (Week 16)

Fill in the numerical values for scoring criteria in the left column. If you are using the default scoring system, the numerical values are listed on Handout 5. If you are using a different scoring system, your teacher will tell you the numerical values. You can get the statistics you need to fill out this handout at www.fantasysportsmath.com.

	QB	RB 1	RB 2	WR 1	WR 2	WR 3	K	Def
Number of TDs × _____								
Number of two-point conversions or safeties × _____								
Number of passing yards (in 25s) × _____								
Number of rushing yards (in 10s) × _____								
Number of receiving yards (in 10s) × _____								
Number of PATs × _____								
Number of FGs × _____								
Number of interceptions × _____								
Number of fumbles lost × _____								
Total individual points								
Total points for the week:								

Weekly Scoring Worksheet (Week 17)

Fill in the numerical values for scoring criteria in the left column. If you are using the default scoring system, the numerical values are listed on Handout 5. If you are using a different scoring system, your teacher will tell you the numerical values. You can get the statistics you need to fill out this handout at www.fantasysportsmath.com.

	QB	RB 1	RB 2	WR 1	WR 2	WR 3	K	Def
Number of TDs × _____								
Number of two-point conversions or safeties × _____								
Number of passing yards (in 25s) × _____								
Number of rushing yards (in 10s) × _____								
Number of receiving yards (in 10s) × _____								
Number of PATs × _____								
Number of FGs × _____								
Number of interceptions × _____								
Number of fumbles lost × _____								
Total individual points								
Total points for the week:								

Weekly Scoring Worksheet Using Total Points Equations (Week 1)

Total points equations are not used to compute points for kickers and defenses. Write the total points equation you are using in the box below. Then compute the points for each of your players. You can get the statistics you need to fill out this handout at www.fantasysportsmath.com.

Player	Computation	Points
QB		
RB1		
WR1		
WR2		
WR3		
K		
Defense		
Total points for the week:		

Weekly Scoring Worksheet Using Total Points Equations (Week 2)

Total points equations are not used to compute points for kickers and defenses. Write the total points equation you are using in the box below. Then compute the points for each of your players. You can get the statistics you need to fill out this handout at www. fantasysportsmath.com.

Player	Computation	Points
QB		
RB1		
WR1		
WR2		
WR3		
K		
Defense		
Total points for the week:		

Weekly Scoring Worksheet Using Total Points Equations (Week 3)

Total points equations are not used to compute points for kickers and defenses. Write the total points equation you are using in the box below. Then compute the points for each of your players. You can get the statistics you need to fill out this handout at www.fantasysportsmath.com.

Player	Computation	Points
QB		
RB1		
WR1		
WR2		
WR3		
K		
Defense		
Total points for the week:		

Weekly Scoring Worksheet Using Total Points Equations (Week 4)

Total points equations are not used to compute points for kickers and defenses. Write the total points equation you are using in the box below. Then compute the points for each of your players. You can get the statistics you need to fill out this handout at www.fantasysportsmath.com.

Player	Computation	Points
QB		
RB1		
WR1		
WR2		
WR3		
K		
Defense		
Total points for the week:		

Weekly Scoring Worksheet Using Total Points Equations (Week 5)

Total points equations are not used to compute points for kickers and defenses. Write the total points equation you are using in the box below. Then compute the points for each of your players. You can get the statistics you need to fill out this handout at www.fantasysportsmath.com.

Player	Computation	Points
QB		
RB1		
WR1		
WR2		
WR3		
K		
Defense		
Total points for the week:		

Peer Signature: _____

Weekly Scoring Worksheet Using Total Points Equations (Week 6)

Total points equations are not used to compute points for kickers and defenses. Write the total points equation you are using in the box below. Then compute the points for each of your players. You can get the statistics you need to fill out this handout at www. fantasysportsmath.com.

Player	Computation	Points
QB		
RB1		
WR1		
WR2		
WR3		
K		
Defense		
Total points for the week:		

Fantasy Football and Mathematics handouts

Weekly Scoring Worksheet Using Total Points Equations (Week 7)

Total points equations are not used to compute points for kickers and defenses. Write the total points equation you are using in the box below. Then compute the points for each of your players. You can get the statistics you need to fill out this handout at www.fantasysportsmath.com.

Player	Computation	Points
QB		
RB1		
WR1		
WR2		
WR3		
K		
Defense		
Total points for the week:		

Weekly Scoring Worksheet Using Total Points Equations (Week 8)

Total points equations are not used to compute points for kickers and defenses. Write the total points equation you are using in the box below. Then compute the points for each of your players. You can get the statistics you need to fill out this handout at www. fantasysportsmath.com.

Player	Computation	Points
QB		
RB1		
WR1		
WR2		
WR3		
K		
Defense		
Total points for the week:		

Fantasy Football and Mathematics handouts

Weekly Scoring Worksheet Using Total Points Equations (Week 9)

Total points equations are not used to compute points for kickers and defenses. Write the total points equation you are using in the box below. Then compute the points for each of your players. You can get the statistics you need to fill out this handout at www.fantasysportsmath.com.

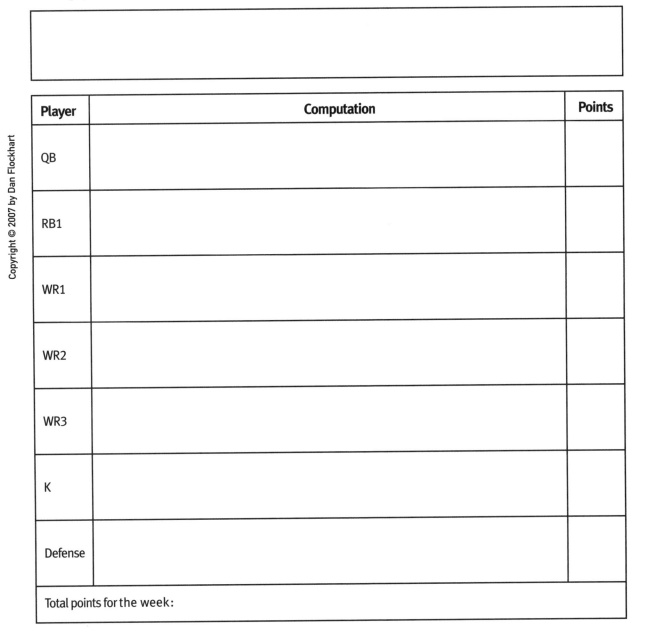

Player	Computation	Points
QB		
RB1		
WR1		
WR2		
WR3		
K		
Defense		
Total points for the week:		

Weekly Scoring Worksheet Using Total Points Equations (Week 10)

Total points equations are not used to compute points for kickers and defenses. Write the total points equation you are using in the box below. Then compute the points for each of your players. You can get the statistics you need to fill out this handout at www. fantasysportsmath.com.

Player	Computation	Points
QB		
RB1		
WR1		
WR2		
WR3		
K		
Defense		
Total points for the week:		

Weekly Scoring Worksheet Using Total Points Equations (Week 11)

Total points equations are not used to compute points for kickers and defenses. Write the total points equation you are using in the box below. Then compute the points for each of your players. You can get the statistics you need to fill out this handout at www.fantasysportsmath.com.

Player	Computation	Points
QB		
RB1		
WR1		
WR2		
WR3		
K		
Defense		
Total points for the week:		

Weekly Scoring Worksheet Using Total Points Equations (Week 12)

Total points equations are not used to compute points for kickers and defenses. Write the total points equation you are using in the box below. Then compute the points for each of your players. You can get the statistics you need to fill out this handout at www. fantasysportsmath.com.

Player	Computation	Points
QB		
RB1		
WR1		
WR2		
WR3		
K		
Defense		
Total points for the week:		

Fantasy Football and Mathematics handouts

Weekly Scoring Worksheet Using Total Points Equations (Week 13)

Total points equations are not used to compute points for kickers and defenses. Write the total points equation you are using in the box below. Then compute the points for each of your players. You can get the statistics you need to fill out this handout at www.fantasysportsmath.com.

Player	Computation	Points
QB		
RB1		
WR1		
WR2		
WR3		
K		
Defense		
Total points for the week:		

Weekly Scoring Worksheet Using Total Points Equations (Week 14)

Total points equations are not used to compute points for kickers and defenses. Write the total points equation you are using in the box below. Then compute the points for each of your players. You can get the statistics you need to fill out this handout at www.fantasysportsmath.com.

Player	Computation	Points
QB		
RB1		
WR1		
WR2		
WR3		
K		
Defense		
Total points for the week:		

Weekly Scoring Worksheet Using Total Points Equations (Week 15)

Total points equations are not used to compute points for kickers and defenses. Write the total points equation you are using in the box below. Then compute the points for each of your players. You can get the statistics you need to fill out this handout at www.fantasysportsmath.com.

Player	Computation	Points
QB		
RB1		
WR1		
WR2		
WR3		
K		
Defense		
Total points for the week:		

Weekly Scoring Worksheet Using Total Points Equations (Week 16)

Total points equations are not used to compute points for kickers and defenses. Write the total points equation you are using in the box below. Then compute the points for each of your players. You can get the statistics you need to fill out this handout at www.fantasysportsmath.com.

Player	Computation	Points
QB		
RB1		
WR1		
WR2		
WR3		
K		
Defense		
Total points for the week:		

Fantasy Football and Mathematics handouts

Weekly Scoring Worksheet Using Total Points Equations (Week 17)

Total points equations are not used to compute points for kickers and defenses. Write the total points equation you are using in the box below. Then compute the points for each of your players. You can get the statistics you need to fill out this handout at www.fantasysportsmath.com.

Player	Computation	Points
QB		
RB1		
WR1		
WR2		
WR3		
K		
Defense		
Total points for the week:		

Total Points Week-by-Week

Team Name: _____   Student Name: _____

Week	QB	RB	RB	WR	WR	WR	K	Def	Weekly Total	Cumulative Total
1										
2										
3										
4										
5										
6										
7										
8										

Fantasy Football and Mathematics handouts

Total Points Week-by-Week *(Cont'd.)*

Team Name: _____   Student Name: _____

Week	QB	RB	RB	WR	WR	WR	K	Def	Weekly Total	Cumulative Total
9										
10										
11										
12										
13										
14										
15										
16										
17										

Graphing Activities

Graphing

Every week, you will construct circle, stacked-bar, or multiple-line graphs.

Circle Graphs

Circle graphs indicate the percentage of the fantasy team's points that each player earns. The equation for computing the measurement of a central angle of a player's portion of the circle is as follows:

$$W \div S \times 360 = A$$

W = total weekly points for one player
S = total weekly points for the team
A = the measurement of the central angle on the circle graph

Figure 3.1. Circle Graph

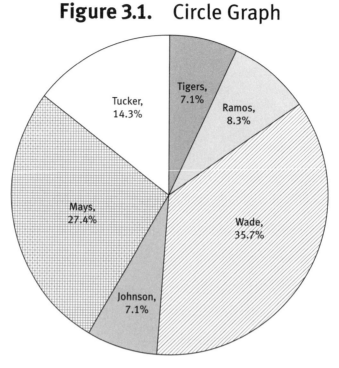

Wildcats Scoring Breakdown, Week 1

Example:

Jesse Wade's total points for week 1 (in simplest form): $\dfrac{5}{8}$

Total points for the Wildcats for Week 1 (in simplest form): $1\dfrac{3}{4}$

Step 1: $\dfrac{5}{8} \div 1\dfrac{3}{4} = \dfrac{5}{8} \div \dfrac{7}{4}$

Step 2: $\dfrac{5}{8} \div \dfrac{7}{4} = \dfrac{5}{8} \times \dfrac{4}{7}$

Step 3: $\dfrac{5}{8} \times \dfrac{4}{7} = \dfrac{20}{56} = \dfrac{5}{14} = .357$ (rounded to nearest 1,000th)

Step 4: $.357 \times 360 = 128.52°$, which rounds to 129°

Figure 3.1 shows a circle graph of the points breakdown for the Wildcats in week 1.

Stacked-Bar and Multiple-Line Graphs

Points earned by individual players can be shown on stacked-bar graphs and multiple-line graphs. A stacked-bar graph is one in which players' weekly points are "stacked" on top of each other. Multiple-line graphs are line graphs that depict the weekly points earned by two or more players. Examples of these graphs are found on the following pages. Intervals of $\frac{1}{48}$, $\frac{2}{48}$, or $\frac{4}{48}$ work well for these graphs, assuming students are using the default scoring system. Students may need to tape additional sheets of graph paper to the top of their first sheet in order to accommodate weeks in which their team scores significant points. My students constructed their graphs by hand, and I gave them extra credit if they created computer-generated charts.

The following pages contain examples of computer-generated graphs. Note that the stacked-bar graph is also used as a handout; its data is used as the basis for activities on several Practice Worksheets.

Stacked-Bar Graph

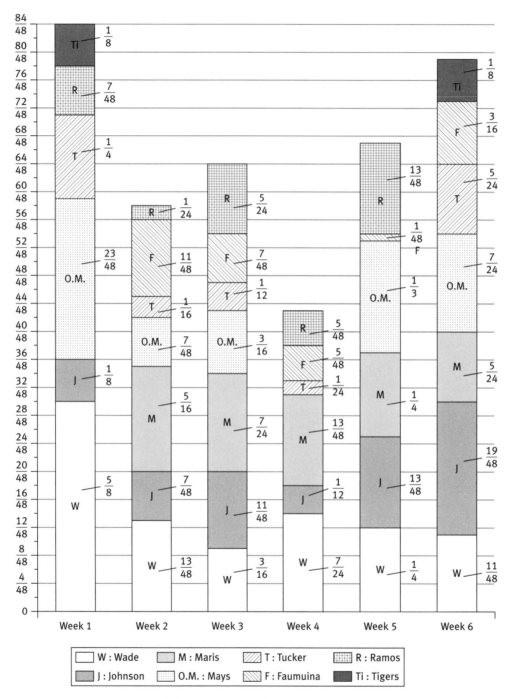

Wildcats Scoring Breakdown, Weeks 1–6

Legend:
- W : Wade
- J : Johnson
- M : Maris
- O.M. : Mays
- T : Tucker
- F : Faumuina
- R : Ramos
- Ti : Tigers

Graphing

Multiple-Line Graph

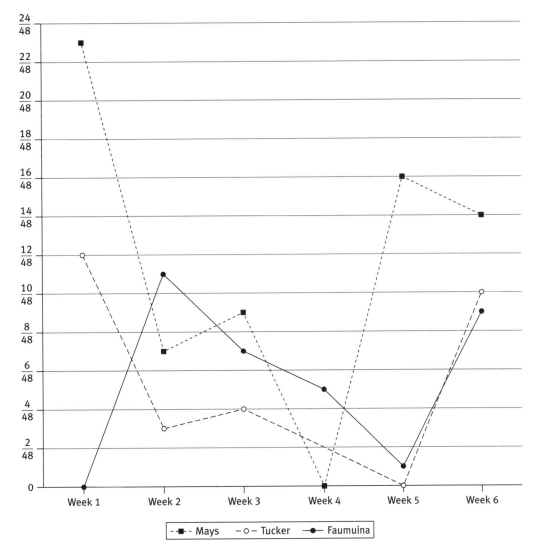

Wildcats Scoring Breakdown, Weeks 1–6

Practice Worksheets

Rounding Whole Numbers and Expanded Notation

1. Round the following player salaries to the units given. The first line gives an example.

Salary	Nearest $10,000	Nearest $100,000	Nearest $1,000,000
$4,884,650	4,880,000	4,900,000	5,000,000
$5,009,900			
$3,555,555			
$2,999,009			
$4,103,737			

2. Use expanded notation to represent the following player salaries. The first line gives an example.

Salary

$6,675,505 = 6,000,000 + 600,000 + 70,000 + 5,000 + 500 + 5

$4,884,650

$5,009,900

$3,555,555

$2,999,009

$4,103,737

Number sense

PRACTICE WORKSHEET 2

Least Common Multiple
and Greatest Common Factor

The weekly points scored by a team for one season are listed below. Find the least common multiple and greatest common factor for each pair of numbers. The first line gives an example.

Weeks	Points Scored	Least Common Multiple	Greatest Common Factor
Weeks 1, 2	7, 21	21	7
Weeks 3, 4	35, 5		
Weeks 5, 6	21, 5		
Weeks 7, 8	10, 30		
Weeks 9, 10	45, 9		

Number sense

Name _____

Operations with Whole Numbers

1. What is the difference between the most expensive and least expensive players listed below?

Player A	$14,007,924
Player B	$14,950,351
Player C	$14,800,995
Player D	$14,675,228
Player E	$14,650,774
Player F	$14,425,005
Player G	$ 3,777,902

2. What is the total cost of the players listed in question 1?

3. What is the average cost of the players listed in question 1, to the nearest dollar?

4. If a player rushed for 1,364 yards in 10 games, how many yards did he average per game?

5. If 14 players each have a salary of $2.7 million, what is the sum of their salaries?

Number sense

PRACTICE WORKSHEET 4

Equivalent Fractions

The points earned by players on the Wildcats are listed below. List the first three equivalent fractions for each.

Jesse Wade	$\frac{5}{8}$	$\frac{10}{16}$	$\frac{15}{24}$	$\frac{20}{32}$
Ty Johnson	$\frac{7}{16}$	_____	_____	_____
Josh Maris	$\frac{2}{3}$	_____	_____	_____
Ollie Mays	$\frac{1}{4}$	_____	_____	_____
D. J. Tucker	$\frac{3}{8}$	_____	_____	_____
Tao Faumuina	$\frac{5}{24}$	_____	_____	_____
Angel Ramos	$\frac{5}{6}$	_____	_____	_____

Number sense

Name _____

PRACTICE WORKSHEET 5
Patterns and Multiples

(Use with Handout 12)

1. Find the first three multiples for the points Jesse Wade earned for week 5. Reduce fractions to simplest form.

2. Find the first three multiples for the points Ty Johnson earned for week 4. Reduce fractions to simplest form.

3. Find the first three multiples for the points earned by Josh Maris for week 2. Reduce fractions to simplest form.

4. If $\frac{60}{48}$ is the third multiple of a number, what is the original number?

5. If 6 is the fourth multiple of a number, what is the original number?

Ordering Fractions and Decimals

(Use with Handout 12)

Example

For week 6, use inequalities to arrange the points earned by players on the Wildcats in ascending order.

$$\frac{6}{48} < \frac{9}{48} < \frac{10}{48} < \frac{10}{48} < \frac{11}{48} < \frac{14}{48} < \frac{19}{48}$$

After converting the fractions to decimals and rounding to the nearest thousandth, you can arrange the decimals in descending order:

$$.396 > .292 > .229 > .208 \geq .208 > .188 > .125$$

Use inequalities to arrange the points earned by players on the Wildcats in descending order for the following weeks. Round decimals to the nearest thousandth.

Week 1

Week 2

Week 3

Week 4

Week 5

Number sense

Name _____

Rounding Decimals

(Use with Handout 12)

Round each player's cumulative points from weeks 1–6 to the nearest tenth, hundredth, and thousandth.

Example

Jesse Wade's cumulative points for Weeks 1–6: $\dfrac{89}{48} = 1\dfrac{41}{48} = 1.8541$

Round to the nearest tenth $= 1.9$

Round to the nearest hundredth $= 1.85$

Round to the nearest thousandth $= 1.854$

Table 1

	Johnson	Maris	Mays	Tucker	Faumuina	Ramos	Tigers
Total Points in Weeks 1–6 (Fraction)							
Total Points in Weeks 1–6 (Decimal)							
Nearest Tenth							
Nearest Hundredth							
Nearest Thousandth							

Use the following table to round the cumulative points for your players for weeks 1–6.

Table 2

Total Points in Weeks 1–6 (Fraction)							
Total Points in Weeks 1–6 (Decimal)							
Nearest Tenth							
Nearest Hundredth							
Nearest Thousandth							

Number sense

Name _____

Improper Fractions, Mixed Numbers, and Reciprocals

The weekly point totals for a team are listed below. Convert all improper fractions to mixed numbers, and write each in its simplest form.

Example

$$\frac{66}{48} = 1\frac{18}{48} = 1\frac{3}{8}$$

1. $\dfrac{79}{48}$

2. $\dfrac{38}{48}$

3. $\dfrac{50}{48}$

4. $\dfrac{106}{48}$

5. $\dfrac{66}{48}$

Write the reciprocals (in simplest form) of the original fractions given in problems 1–5.

6.

7.

8.

9.

10.

Name _____

Adding and Subtracting Fractions

(Use with Handout 12)

Example

For week 5, find the sum of the points earned by Josh Maris, Ollie Mays, and Tao Faumuina.

$$\frac{12}{48} + \frac{16}{48} + \frac{1}{48} = \frac{29}{48}$$

1. For week 3, find the sum of the points earned by Jesse Wade, Ty Johnson, and Ollie Mays.

2. For week 2, find the sum of the points earned by the Wildcats, with the exception of Angel Ramos and Josh Maris.

3. Find the sum of the points earned by Ollie Mays and Jesse Wade for weeks 1–5.

4. Find the sum of the points earned by all players for weeks 1–3, with the exception of Jesse Wade and Ollie Mays.

5. For week 4, find the sum of the points earned by all players, with the exception of Ty Johnson and Angel Ramos.

Number sense

Name _____

Stacked–Bar Graphs

(Use with Handout 12)

Using graph paper and an interval of $\frac{4}{48}$, construct a stacked-bar graph based on the data below. *Hint:* Convert all fractions so that they have a common denominator.

Player	Week 1	Week 2	Week 3
QB	$\frac{5}{12}$	$\frac{1}{2}$	$\frac{29}{48}$
RB	$\frac{7}{16}$	$\frac{19}{48}$	$\frac{5}{12}$
WR	$\frac{1}{16}$	$\frac{1}{3}$	$\frac{3}{8}$

Number sense

Copyright © 2007 by Dan Flockhart

PRACTICE WORKSHEET 11

Multiplying and Dividing Fractions

1. How many weeks would it take a player to earn $5\frac{33}{48}$ points if he averaged $\frac{7}{16}$ points a week?

2. If D. J. Tucker earned $\frac{1}{16}$ points and Ollie Mays earned $\frac{7}{48}$ points, what is the product of their points earned?

3. The product of the points that Jesse Wade and Ollie Mays earned is $\frac{27}{128}$. If Wade earned $\frac{9}{16}$ points, how many points did Mays earn?

4. A player earned $12\frac{16}{48}$ points during a 16-game season. How many points did he average per week?

5. If Marvin Samuels earned $2\frac{1}{8}$ points for the season, and Reggie Blackmon earned $\frac{7}{16}$ for each week, how many weeks would it take Blackmon to match Samuels's points?

Number sense

PRACTICE WORKSHEET 12

Rounding Fractions

(Use with Handout 12)

1. In Table 1, round the players' cumulative points from weeks 1–6 to the nearest $\frac{1}{2}$, $\frac{1}{4}$, and $\frac{1}{8}$.

Example

Ollie Mays's cumulative points for weeks 1–6 $= \frac{69}{48} = 1\frac{21}{48} = 1\frac{7}{16}$

Round to the nearest $\frac{1}{2} = 1\frac{1}{2}$

Round to the nearest $\frac{1}{4} = 1\frac{1}{2}$

Round to the nearest $\frac{1}{8} = 1\frac{1}{2}$

Table 1

	Wade	**Johnson**	**Maris**	**Tucker**	**Faumuina**	**Ramos**	**Tigers**
Nearest $\frac{1}{2}$							
Nearest $\frac{1}{4}$							
Nearest $\frac{1}{8}$							

Use the following table to round the cumulative points for your players for weeks 1–6.

Table 2

Player							
Nearest $\frac{1}{2}$							
Nearest $\frac{1}{4}$							
Nearest $\frac{1}{8}$							

Number sense

Name _____

Multiplying and Dividing Decimals

1. If a quarterback had annual quarterback ratings of 88.64, 101.88, 76.75, 90.09, and 93.53, what would be his average rating for the past five years?

2. If Doug Jones worked 8 hours a day, 175 days a year, and his annual salary was $4.4 million, how much money did he make each working day? Each working hour? Each working minute? Each working second? Round your answers to the nearest cent.

3. If a snail can crawl at a rate of .07 yards per minute, how many hours will it take the snail to crawl the length of a football field (100 yards)? One mile?

4. If 60,000 fans each consumed an average of 7.75 ounces of soda at each game, how many ounces of soda were consumed for 14 games? How many 12 ounce sodas were consumed?

5. If a vendor selling ice cream sandwiches works 4 hours at $7.50 an hour and also receives 35 cents for each sandwich sold, what is her income if she sold 323 sandwiches?

Number sense

Name _____

Unit Rates

Example

At a football game, you can purchase 16 ounces of soda for $2.75 or 24 ounces for $4.00. Which size is the lower price per ounce?

$2.75 ÷ 16 ounces = 17.2 cents per ounce

$4.00 ÷ 24 ounces = 16.7 cents per ounce (lowest price per ounce)

The 24-ounce size has the lower price per ounce.

1. If you can purchase 12 ounces of peanuts for $3.75 or 20 ounces for $5.75, what is the cost for the lower price per ounce?

2. If Susan Haines drove her car 300 miles on 30 gallons of gas and Chrissy Dolling drove her car 450 miles on 15 gallons of gas, what is the miles per gallon for each car?

3. If Jessica Williams can purchase 50 acres for $2.5 million or 75 acres for $3.5 million, what is the cost of the lower price per acre?

4. If you can purchase a 10-game season ticket for $450 or a 1-game ticket for $55, which is the lower price per game?

5. Which is the higher salary per year: $4.5 million for 8 years or $8.5 million for 15 years?

Number sense

Name _____

Converting Fractions, Decimals, and Percentages

(Use with Handout 12)

1. Find the cumulative points for each player, and convert the fractions into decimals. Then round to the nearest tenth, hundredth, and thousandth. Finally, convert all decimals to a percentage, rounded to the nearest tenth.

Player	Total Points (Fraction)	Total Points (Decimal)	Rounded to Nearest Tenth	Rounded to Nearest Hundredth	Rounded to Nearest Thousandth	Percentage (Rounded to Nearest Tenth)
Wade	$1\frac{41}{48}$	1.8542	1.9	1.85	1.854	185.4%
Johnson						
Maris						
Mays						
Tucker						

2. Fill in the table below for the cumulative points for your team for the first six weeks.

Your Player	Total Points (Fraction)	Total Points (Decimal)	Rounded to Nearest Tenth	Rounded to Nearest Hundredth	Rounded to Nearest Thousandth	Percentage (Rounded to Nearest Tenth)
QB						
RB1						
RB2						
WR1						
WR2						
WR3						

Number sense

Name _____

Ratios

(Use with Handout 12)

Example

$$\frac{\text{Total points for Mays, Tucker, and Faumuina}}{\text{Total points for Wade}} = \frac{17}{12} = 1.41\overline{6} = 141.7\%$$

For week 5, find the following ratios, and convert them to percentages.

1. $\dfrac{\text{Total points for Johnson and Maris}}{\text{Total points for Mays, Tucker, and Faumuina}}$

2. $\dfrac{\text{Total points for Wade}}{\text{Total points for Ramos}}$

3. $\dfrac{\text{Total points for Ramos, Tigers, Johnson, and Maris}}{\text{Total points for Mays, Tucker, Faumuina, and Wade}}$

For week 6, find the following ratios, and convert them to percentages.

4. $\dfrac{\text{Total points for Johnson, Maris, and Ramos}}{\text{Total points for Wade, Mays, Tucker, and Faumunia}}$

5. $\dfrac{\text{Total points for Mays, Tucker, and Faumuina}}{\text{Total points for Johnson and Maris}}$

Number sense

Name _____

Percentage of Price Increase and Decrease

Example

If the price of a football jersey rose from $42 to $54, what is the percentage of price increase?

$$\frac{\text{Change in Price}}{\text{Original Price}} = \frac{12}{42} = 19.8\% \text{ increase}$$

1. If the price of an autographed football rose from $155 to $225, what is the percentage of price increase?

2. If the price of a football video game decreased from $85 to $75, what is the percentage of price decrease?

3. If the price of a season ticket decreased from $675 to $555, what is the percentage of price decrease?

4. If the price of a season ticket increased from $465 to $770, what is the percentage of price increase?

5. If a player's salary increased from $13 million to $16.5 million, what percentage increase would that represent?

Number sense

Name _____

Finding a Percentage of a Number

Example

Ollie Mays earned $\frac{7}{48}$ points. What percentage of André Young's points $\left(\frac{15}{48}\right)$ does this represent?

$$n \times \left(\frac{15}{48}\right) = \frac{7}{48}$$

$$\text{therefore, } n = \frac{7}{48} \div \left(\frac{15}{48}\right)$$

$$\text{thus, } n = \frac{7}{15} = .4\overline{6} = 47\%$$

1. Tim Dunfield earned $\frac{6}{48}$ points. What percentage of Larue Jones's points $\left(\frac{18}{48}\right)$ does this represent?

2. Drew Lane earned $\frac{7}{48}$ points. What percentage of Edgar Palmer's points $\left(\frac{13}{48}\right)$ does this represent?

3. What percentage of Dan Banning's points $\left(\frac{31}{48}\right)$ do Greg Foster's points $\left(\frac{13}{48}\right)$ represent?

4. Curt Brock earned $\frac{16}{48}$ points, which was 80% of Michael Smith's points. How many points did Smith earn?

5. Jesse Wade earned $\frac{1}{8}$ points, which was 60% of Ollie Mays's points. How many points did Mays earn?

Number sense

Finding a Percentage of a Number *(Cont'd.)*

6. Rod Blanchard earned $\frac{3}{4}$ points, which was 120% of Kevan Williams's points. How many points did Williams earn?

7. If Mike Dillion earned 150% of his week 8 point total $(\frac{6}{48})$, how many points did he earn?

8. There are 80,000 football fans in Oakland and 56,000 baseball fans in San Francisco. Each year, 20% of the football fans move to San Francisco, and 15% of the baseball fans move to Oakland. Complete the table below.

After Year	Baseball Fans in Oakland	Football Fans in San Francisco
1		
2		
3		
4		

Number sense

Name _____

Proportions

Example

If a player earned $1\frac{6}{24}$ points during the first 4 weeks of the season, how many points is he projected to earn for an entire 16-game season?

$$\frac{1.25}{4} = \frac{n}{16}$$

$$1.25(16) = 4n$$

$$n = 5$$

1. If a player earned $1\frac{5}{16}$ points during the first 7 weeks of the season, how many points is he projected to earn in a 16-game season?

2. If it took a player 3 weeks to earn $\frac{7}{16}$ points, how many weeks would it take him to earn $4\frac{1}{8}$ points?

3. If it took a player 12 weeks to earn $2\frac{1}{48}$ points, how many weeks would it take him to earn 10 points?

4. A player earned $2\frac{8}{12}$ points for the entire season. If he earned an equal number of points each week, how many points did he accumulate after 9 weeks?

Number sense

Proportions *(Cont'd.)*

5. A player earned 2 points for the entire season. If he earned an equal number of points each week, how many points would he have accumulated after 7 weeks?

6. If a player threw for 1,434 yards during the first 5 games, then how many passing yards is he projected to accumulate in a 16-game season?

7. A player gained 357 yards rushing during the first 3 games. If he maintains his current pace, how many rushing yards will he accumulate through 10 games?

8. An architect is constructing a scale drawing of a new stadium. On the scale, 1 inch represents 20 feet. If the actual length of the football field is 300 feet, what is the length of the football field on the scale drawing?

9. In problem 8, what would be the actual height of the goal posts if the scale drawing showed a height of 2 inches?

10. If it took 33 hours to drive 2,000 miles nonstop, how long would it take to drive 3,000 miles nonstop assuming that the average speed remained constant on both trips?

PRACTICE WORKSHEET 20

Ratios and Proportions

Example

During week 4, the ratio of Ron Harris's points to Ben Willis's points was 3:1. If Harris earned $\frac{21}{48}$ points that week, how many points did Willis earn?

$$\frac{3}{1} = \frac{\dfrac{21}{48}}{n}$$

$$3n = \frac{21}{48}$$

$$n = \frac{7}{48}$$

1. During week 14, the ratio of Jeff McQueen's points to Trey Williamson's points was 4:3. If Williamson earned $\frac{12}{48}$ points, how many points did McQueen earn?

2. During week 12, the ratio of Cory Chavas's points to Tony Packney's points was 1:3. If Packney earned $\frac{24}{48}$ points, how many points did Chavas earn?

3. During week 13, the ratio of Ollie Mays's points to Jesse Wade's points was 5:2. If Mays earned $\frac{30}{48}$ points, how many points did Wade earn?

4. During week 14, the ratio of David Benson's points to Jim Price's points was 6:5. If Price earned $\frac{25}{48}$, how many points did Benson earn?

5. During week 10, the ratio of Jerry Gates's points to Chris Jillian's points was 13:21. If Jillian earned $\frac{7}{8}$ points, how many points did Gates earn?

Number sense

Name _____

Factoring

Example

The product of the points earned by Harry Rincot for weeks 1 and 2 is $\frac{18}{48}$. If Rincot earned $\frac{3}{12}$ points for week 1, how many points did he earn for week 2?

$$\frac{3}{12} \times \frac{\square}{\square} = \frac{18}{48}$$

$$n = \frac{6}{4} = 1\frac{1}{2}$$

1. The product of the points earned by two players for week 8 is $\frac{44}{48}$. If one player earned $\frac{11}{12}$ points, how many points did the second player earn?

2. With the exception of 1, find two factors whose product equals $1\frac{18}{48}$.

3. The area of a table tennis table is 45 square feet. If the length and width are whole numbers, what are the only two realistic factors for the table's dimensions?

4. One factor of $\frac{32}{45}$ is $\frac{4}{9}$. Find a second factor.

5. Find a second factor if one factor of $\frac{24}{48}$ is 4.

Number sense

PRACTICE WORKSHEET 22

Interest, Depreciation, and Tax

1. If a player signed an eight-year contract for $105,000,000 and invested 45% of his annual salary at a rate of 6.25% for each year, how much interest will he earn at the end of 2 years if the interest is compounded annually? (Assume that his income remains constant during the life of the contract.) Construct a spreadsheet showing the interest earned and total value of his account at the end of each year. Use the following formula:

I = PRT
I = interest earned
P = principle
R = interest rate
T = time

2. If a player purchases a car for $150,000, and the state sales tax rate is 8.5%, how much tax will he owe? What will be the total cost of the car?

3. If the value of the automobile depreciates by 10% each year, what will the car be worth at the end of 3 years? Construct a spreadsheet showing the amount of depreciation and corresponding value of the car each year.

4. If a player purchased a house for $8,500,000, and the price of the home appreciates 10% a year for the next 2 years, what will be the value of the home at the end of that period? Construct a spreadsheet showing the amount of annual appreciation and corresponding value of the house at the end of each year.

Number sense

Name _____

Prime Factorization

Below are the weekly point totals (in 48ths) for a team. Write the prime factorization of each number using exponential notation. The first row is filled in as an example.

Week	*Point Totals*	*Prime Factorization*
Week 1	66	$2 \times 3 \times 11$
Week 2	79	
Week 3	38	
Week 4	50	
Week 5	106	
Week 6	66	
Week 7	69	

List the first five prime numbers: ____   ____   ____   ____   ____

Number sense

PRACTICE WORKSHEET 24

Scientific Notation

The dimensions of a football field are 300 feet by 160 feet. Write the area of the field in scientific notation for the following units of measurement. *Hint*: 1 in. = 2.5 cm.

Example

Square feet   Area = 48,000 sq. feet = 4.8×10^4

    1. Square inches

    2. Square yards

    3. Square centimeters

    4. Square millimeters

    5. Square meters

    6. 26.75

    7. .000005

    8. .000777

    9. 877,887.5665

  10. 1,000,000.7

Write the following in standard form.

  11. 9.002×10^{-2}

  12. $\dfrac{15}{48} \times 10^3$

     Number sense

Name _____

Ordering Integers, Fractions, and Decimals

1. The following integers represent the temperatures for several cities in December. Place them in ascending order on the number line below.

45   −3   −21   −17   −9   −32   21   76   44   −1   11

2. The following integers represent the rushing yards gained or lost by a quarterback during the first 10 games of the season. Place them in ascending order on the number line below.

−34   12   7   21   −55   −33   −3   −41   41   −2

3. Place the following numerical values on the number line in ascending order.

$-.011998$ $4\frac{2}{5}$ $-5\frac{5}{16}$ -2.888 7.004 $-3\frac{7}{8}$

4. Place the following numerical values on the number line in ascending order.

$.125$ $\frac{1}{3}$ $\frac{11}{48}$ $\frac{7}{48}$ $\frac{3}{16}$ $\frac{1}{6}$

Name _____

Operations with Integers

1. If a quarterback lost 5,553 yards rushing over the course of 15 seasons, how many yards did he lose on average per season?

2. The numerical values below represent the rushing totals for 10 running backs. How many total yards did they rush for?

   -16 126 -3 19   167 -22 -41 -5 -33 65

3. If a running back rushed for -13 yards in the first game of the season, how many yards is he projected to lose for a complete 16-game season?

4. If Tony Reno gained 112 yards in the first game of the season, how many yards is he projected to gain for a complete 16-game season?

Number sense

Operations with Integers *(Cont'd.)*

5. The numbers below represent profit or loss for five teams for one year. What is the average profit or loss?

   −$445,000 $4,987,435   −$3,722,256   −$66,773 $25,776,232

6. If one team lost $1,978,330 while another team reported a profit of $22,656,944, how much greater was the second team's profit compared to the other team's loss?

7. If one team reported a loss of $13,111,008, which included a profit of $1,777,456 on parking fees, how much money did it lose on operations other than parking fees?

Name _____

Permutations and Combinations

1. There are eight running backs on a team. If the coach started two running backs, how many combinations could he choose from?

2. If a team has jerseys in three different styles, helmets in two different styles, and pants in three different styles, how many combinations of uniforms are there to choose from?

3. A team's uniform consists of two colors, but they have five colors to choose from. How many combinations of uniforms do they have?

4. Before a game, eight referees line up in single file for the National Anthem. In how many ways can the referees line up in single file?

Number sense

Name _____

Unit Conversions

1. The length of a football field is 100 yards. What is the length of a field in inches? In centimeters? (2.5 centimeters = 1 inch)

2. A player gained 125 yards rushing. How many feet did he gain?

3. The width of a football field is 160 feet. What is the width of the field in yards?

4. If the length of a football field is 10,800 inches, find its length in millimeters. *Hint:* 10 mm = 1 cm

5. A team spent 4,200 minutes practicing last week. How many hours did they spend practicing?

6. A team is scheduled to play their next game in exactly 3 days, 4 hours. How many hours until they play their next game? How many minutes?

Algebra and functions   93

Evaluating Algebraic Expressions

Evaluate $\frac{1}{8}(T) + \frac{1}{24}(V) + \frac{1}{48}(P + R + C) - \frac{1}{12}(I) - \frac{1}{16}(F)$ if

1. $T = 2$
   $V = 1$
   $P = 14$
   $R = 3$
   $C = 0$
   $I = 2$
   $F = 0$

2. $T = 3$
   $V = 0$
   $P = 1$
   $R = 17$
   $C = 7$
   $I = 4$
   $F = 1$

Evaluate $\left(\dfrac{W}{S}\right) 360$ if:

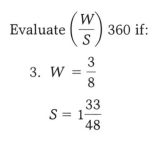

3. $W = \dfrac{3}{8}$

   $S = 1\dfrac{33}{48}$

4. $W = \dfrac{1}{2}$

   $S = 2\dfrac{1}{2}$

Algebra and functions

Name _____

Properties of Mathematics

Distributive property	$a(b + c) = ab + ac$
Commutative property of addition	$a + b = b + a$
Commutative property of multiplication	$ab = ba$
Associative property of addition	$a + (b + c) = (a + b) + c$
Associative property of multiplication	$a(bc) = (ab)c$
Inverse property of addition	$a + (-a) = 0$
Inverse property of multiplication	$a \times \dfrac{1}{a} = 1$
Identity property of addition	$a + 0 = a$
Identity property of multiplication	$a(1) = a$

The following equations are used to compute the points earned in various Fantasy sports. List the mathematical property of each, and fill in the missing term.

1. $\dfrac{7}{48}C + \dfrac{1}{2}R + \dfrac{3}{8}P = \dfrac{1}{2}R + \dfrac{3}{8}P +$ _____

   Property: _____

2. $\dfrac{2}{21}R \times \dfrac{3}{11}C = \dfrac{3}{11}C \times$ _____

   Property: _____

3. $\dfrac{3}{5}\left(P + \dfrac{1}{2}\right) = \dfrac{3}{5}P +$ _____

   Property: _____

Properties of Mathematics *(Cont'd.)*

4. $\dfrac{3}{24}R + \left(\dfrac{1}{4}C + \dfrac{2}{5}P\right) = $ _____ $\left(\dfrac{3}{24}R + \text{___}\right) + \dfrac{2}{5}P$

   Property: _____

5. $\dfrac{1}{5}P \times \left(\dfrac{3}{10}C \times \dfrac{2}{9}R\right) = $ _____ $\left(- \times \dfrac{3}{10}C\right) \times \dfrac{2}{9}R$

   Property: _____

6. $\dfrac{9}{48}C + ($ _____ $) = 0$

   Property: _____

7. $\dfrac{5}{12}P(0) = $ _____

   Property: _____

8. $2\dfrac{1}{8} + $ _____ $= 2\dfrac{1}{8}$

   Property: _____

9. _____ $(1) = \dfrac{31}{48}$

   Property: _____

Algebra and functions

Name _____

Graphing on a Number Line

(Use with Handout 12)

Example

During the first six weeks, Jesse Wade's range of points earned was between and $\frac{9}{48}$ and $\frac{30}{48}$, inclusive. Using these data, we can graph the range of points earned by Wade on a number line.

$$\overset{\bullet\rule{3cm}{0.4pt}\bullet}{\underset{\dfrac{9}{48}\qquad\quad\dfrac{30}{48}}{}}$$

Use a number line to graph the range of points earned from weeks 1–6 for the following players.

1. Ty Johnson _____

2. Josh Maris _____

3. Ollie Mays _____

4. D. J. Tucker _____

5. Tao Faumuina _____

6. Tigers _____

Algebra and functions

Linear Equations (A)

The equations below are used to compute total weekly points or to find the measurement of central angles in a circle graph. In each case, solve for the variable.

1. $\dfrac{1}{8}(3) + \dfrac{1}{24}(1) + \dfrac{1}{48}(P + 5 + 12) - \dfrac{1}{12}(0) - \dfrac{1}{16}(2) = \dfrac{11}{16}$

2. $\dfrac{1}{8}(4) + \dfrac{1}{24}(0) + \dfrac{1}{48}(15 + R + 8) - \dfrac{1}{12}(2) - \dfrac{1}{16}(1) = \dfrac{13}{16}$

3. $\dfrac{1}{8}(2) + \dfrac{1}{24}(1) + \dfrac{1}{48}(0 + 1 + C) - \dfrac{1}{12}(0) - \dfrac{1}{16}(2) = \dfrac{9}{16}$

4. $\dfrac{1}{8}(T) + \dfrac{1}{24}(0) + \dfrac{1}{48}(7 + 3 + 0) - \dfrac{1}{12}(3) - \dfrac{1}{16}(2) = \dfrac{1}{8}$

5. $w \div 4 \times 360 = 180$

Algebra and functions

Linear Equations (A) *(Cont'd.)*

6. $\dfrac{w}{3} \times 360 = 40$

7. $\dfrac{1}{8} \div s \times 360 = 30$

8. $\dfrac{1}{2} \div 2.5 \times 360 = A$

9. $\dfrac{w}{2.25} \times 360 = 90$

10. $.6^0\,(3) + .6^{-1}\,(0) + .6^{-2}\,(0 + 4 + C) - .6^{-3}\,(0) - .6^{-4}\,(1) = 25.84$

Algebra and functions

Linear Equations (A) *(Cont'd.)*

11. $2^4 (2) + 2^2 (V) + 2^3 (7 + 1 + 0) - 2^4 (2) - 2^5 (1) = 8$

12. $4^{-1} (T) + 4^{-2} (0) + 4^{-3} (0 + 8 + 8) - 4^{-4} (0) - 4^{-5} (0) = 1$

13. $\left(\sum\limits_{j=1}^{6} j \right) (1) + \left(\sum\limits_{j=1}^{5} j \right) (0) + \left(\sum\limits_{j=1}^{4} j \right) (2 + R + 2) - \left(\sum\limits_{j=1}^{3} j \right) (0) - \left(\sum\limits_{j=1}^{2} j \right) (1) = 79$

14. $6! (2) + 5! (1) + 4! (0 + 10 + C) - 3! (1) - 2! (2) = 1958$

Algebra and functions

15. $\dfrac{5}{6}$ (4) $+ \dfrac{4}{5}$ (0) $+ \dfrac{3}{4}$ (10 + 2 + 2) $- \dfrac{2}{7}$ (*I*) $- \dfrac{2}{8}$ (0) $= 13.5476$

16. $\left(\dfrac{5}{6}\right)^0$ (*T*) $+ \left(\dfrac{4}{5}\right)^1$ (1) $+ \left(\dfrac{3}{4}\right)^2$ (8 + 5 + 0) $- \left(\dfrac{2}{7}\right)^3$ (0) $- \left(\dfrac{1}{4}\right)^4$ (2) $= 11.1046875$

17. $-.075$ (2) $- .025$ (0) $- .0125$ (16 + 2 + 0) $+ .05$ (0) $+ .0375$ (*F*) $= -.3$

18. $.06$ (0) $+ .02$ (0) $+ .01$ (0 + 0 + 4) $- .04$ (*I*) $- .03$ (3) $= -.09$

Name _____

Linear Equations (B)

In the problems below, insert the values shown for each variable in the total points equation. Then solve for W, and write the answer in its simplest form.

$$\frac{1}{8}(T) + \frac{1}{24}(V) + \frac{1}{48}(P + R + C) - \frac{1}{12}(I) - \frac{1}{16}(F) = W$$

1. $P = 3$
   $R = 2$
   $C = 4$
   $T = 3$
   $V = 1$
   $I = 4$
   $F = 2$
   $W =$

2. $P = 7$
   $C = 4$
   $T = 2$
   $R = 5$
   $V = 2$
   $I = 1$
   $F = 3$
   $W =$

3. $R = 3$
   $P = 11$
   $C = 7$
   $V = 0$
   $T = 4$
   $I = 2$
   $F = 2$
   $W =$

Algebra and functions

Name _____

Area and Perimeter of Rectangles

1. Explain the meaning of the variables in the following equations:

$$P = 2l + 2w$$

$$A = bh$$

2. The rectangular dimensions of a professional football field are 160 by 360 feet. This includes the end zones, each of which is 30 feet in length. The width and length of a junior field (for younger players) is 100 feet by 180 feet. Find the area and perimeter of both football fields. Then find the ratio of the area of the professional field to the area of the junior field in each measurement unit. Do you see any patterns? Explain your answer.

	Area of Professional Field	Area of Junior Field	Ratio of Area of Professional Field to Area of Junior Field
Square feet			
Square inches			
Square yards			
Square centimeters (2.5 cm. = 1 inch)			
Square millimeters			
Square meters			

3. If artificial turf costs $35 per square foot, how much would it cost to resurface a field, including the end zones?

Area and Perimeter of Rectangles *(Cont'd.)*

4. How much would it cost to resurface the junior field if the price of artificial turf was $20 per square foot?

5. Find the perimeter of a professional football field, a soccer field, a professional basketball court, and a high school basketball court. Then make two statements comparing the areas of any two of the playing surfaces. For example, you may predict that a football field is three times larger than a basketball court, or that a soccer field is 25% larger than a rugby field. Then find the actual area, and see how close your predictions were.

Statement 1:

Statement 2:

Playing Surface	Dimensions	Area	Perimeter
Professional football field	300 ft. by 160 ft.		
Soccer field	68 m by 105 m		
Professional basketball court	94 ft. by 50 ft.		
High school basketball court	84 ft. by 45 ft.		

Measurement and geometry

Name _____

PRACTICE WORKSHEET 35
Golden Rectangles

A Golden Rectangle is a rectangle in which the ratio of its length to its width is about 1.6:1.

1. Fill in the chart below.

	Dimensions	Ratio of Length to Width	Difference from Golden Rectangle Ratio
Professional basketball court	94 ft. by 50 ft.		
Football field	300 ft. by 160 ft.		
College/high school basketball court	84 ft. by 50 ft.		
Soccer field	105 m. by 68 m.		
Junior basketball court	74 ft. by 42 ft.		

2. Which playing surfaces have a ratio that approximates that of a Golden Rectangle?

3. Measure the length and width of various objects to find examples of Golden Rectangles. Some suggestions: flags, calculators, books, blackboards, windows, doors, file cabinets.

4. Predict the ratio of your height to the span of your two arms. Find the ratio. What did you learn?

Measurement and geometry

105

PRACTICE WORKSHEET 36

Functions

In the exercises below, (1) write the function rule and (2) solve for the variable.

1. X = number of touchdowns; Y = points earned.

Function rule: _____

X	Y
1	$\frac{6}{48}$
2	$\frac{12}{48}$
3	$\frac{18}{48}$
7	n

2. X = number of rushing yards in sets of 10; Y = points earned.

Function rule: _____

X	Y
1	$\frac{1}{48}$
3	$\frac{3}{48}$
5	$\frac{5}{48}$
13	n

Measurement and geometry

Functions *(Cont'd.)*

3. X = number of field goals; Y = number of points earned.

   Function rule: _____

X	Y
7	$\dfrac{7}{16}$
14	$\dfrac{14}{16}$
21	$\dfrac{21}{16}$
35	n

4. Construct your own function chart below.

   Function rule: _____

X	Y

Measurement and geometry

Name _____

Area and Circumference of Circles

Area of circle $= \pi r^2$

Circumference of circle $= \pi d$

r = radius; d = diameter; $\pi = 3.14$

1. A circular logo located at the center of the football field has a diameter of 38 feet. Find the area and circumference of the logo.

2. If the area of a logo is 100.48 square feet, what is the diameter of the logo?

3. If a circular logo has a diameter of 15 feet, what is the area of the logo?

4. On a basketball court, the circle at the center of the court has a radius of 4 feet. Find the diameter, circumference, and area of the circle.

Diameter: _____

Circumference: _____

Area: _____

5. If the circumference of a logo on a shirt is 5 inches, what are the radius, diameter, and area of the logo?

Radius: _____

Diameter: _____

Area: _____

Measurement and geometry

PRACTICE WORKSHEET 38

Weight

Predict and then find the weight of the following objects, in the given units. You will need a scale.

	Predicted Weight			Actual Weight		
	Pounds	Ounces	Grams	Pounds	Ounces	Grams
Football						
Basketball						
Baseball						
Soccer ball						
Table tennis ball						
Hockey puck						

For each of the following problems, predict the answer, then solve the problem.

1. How many table tennis balls would weigh as much as a football? As much as a tennis ball? As much as a hockey puck?

2. Which is greater: the weight of 3 hockey pucks or 7 basketballs?

3. Which is less: the weight of 1,000 table tennis balls or 10 footballs?

4. How many table tennis balls would it take to equal your body weight? How many soccer balls?

Measurement and geometry

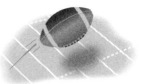

PRACTICE WORKSHEET 39

Pythagorean Theorem

In a right triangle,

$$a^2 + b^2 = c^2$$

where

  a = length of one leg of the triangle
  b = length of the other leg of the triangle
  c = length of the hypotenuse

Use the Pythagorean Theorem to solve the following problems:

1. The distance between consecutive bases on a baseball diamond is 30 yards. Find the distance from first base to third base.

2. Find the length of the diagonal of a football field if the length is 300 feet and the width is 160 feet.

3. Find the length of the diagonal of a basketball court if the length is 94 feet and the width is 50 feet.

4. Find the width of a soccer field if the length is 105 meters and the length of the diagonal is 125 meters.

5. Find the width of a lacrosse field if the length of the field is 112 yards and the length of the diagonal is 133 yards.

Measurement and geometry

Name _____

Mean, Median, Mode, and Range

(Use with Handout 12)

1. For each of the first six weeks, find the points earned by each player on the Wildcats. In the table below, record the mean, median, mode, and range for the points earned for each of the first six weeks.

Week	Mean	Median	Mode	Range
1				
2				
3				
4				
5				
6				

2. For each of the first six weeks, find the points earned by each player on your team. In the table below, record the mean, median, mode, and range of the points earned for each of the first six weeks.

Week	Mean	Median	Mode	Range
1				
2				
3				
4				
5				
6				

Statistics, data analysis, and probability

Probability

1. Last year, a quarterback threw 25% of his passes to the left side of the field, 35% to the right side, and 40% straight downfield. If the quarterback attempted 600 passes last year, how many passes did he throw in each direction?

2. Using only the data in problem 1, what is the probability that the quarterback's first pass this year will be to his left side?

3. A team's record during the past 10 years is 90–70. Without taking any other variables into account, what should the team's record be this year?

4. In how many ways can you express the outcome if the probability that an event will occur is 25%? *Hint:* $\frac{1}{4}$.

5. If the probability that an event will occur is 55%, what is the probability that the event will not occur?

Statistics, data analysis, and probability

Probability *(Cont'd.)*

6. The letters in "Gar Jendvat" are placed into a hat. Find the probability of the following random events.

   A. Selecting the letter *v*

   B. Selecting the letters *d, e,* or *r*

   C. Selecting the letter *z*

   D. Selecting any letter except *r*

   E. Selecting the letter *g,* replacing it, then selecting the letter *g* again

   F. Selecting the letters *d* and *j* on consecutive draws (without replacing letters)

In exercises 7–11, you are given $P(Q)$, the probability that a player will rush for 100 yards in a given game. Find $P(\text{not } Q)$, the probability that event Q will not occur.

7. $P(Q) = \dfrac{27}{48}$ $\qquad$ $P(\text{not } Q) =$

8. $P(Q) = .435$ $\qquad$ $P(\text{not } Q) =$

9. $P(Q) = 39\%$ $\qquad$ $P(\text{not } Q) =$

10. $P(Q) = 1$ $\qquad$ $P(\text{not } Q) =$

11. $P(Q) = 0$ $\qquad$ $P(\text{not } Q) =$

PRACTICE WORKSHEET 42

Circle Graphs

(Use with Handout 12)

$W \div S \times 360 = A$

W = total weekly points for one player
S = total weekly points for the team
A = the measurement of the central angle of the circle graph

Example

In week 4, Jesse Wade earned $\frac{14}{48}$ points. Find the measurement of the central angle representing Wade's portion of his team's total points for that week.

$$\frac{14}{48} \div \frac{43}{48} \times 360 = 117.2°$$

1. Find the measurement of the central angles for all players on the Wildcats for week 4.

2. Find the measurement of the central angles for all players on the Wildcats for week 5.

3. Find the measurement of the central angles showing the cumulative points for the players on the Wildcats for weeks 1–6.

4. If the central angle in a circle graph is 30 degrees, what percentage of the graph will that section represent?

5. If the central angle in a circle graph is 45 degrees, what percentage of the graph will that section represent?

6. If one section of a circle graph represented 75% of the total graph, what is the measurement of the corresponding central angle?

7. The sum of the percentages inside a circle graph is 359 degrees. Explain how this could occur.

Statistics, data analysis, and probability

Name _____

Stem-and-Leaf Plots and Histograms

1. The following values represent the weekly point totals (in 48ths) for the Wildcats for a 16-game season. Using graph paper, construct a stem-and-leaf plot and histogram.

66	79	38	50	106	66	69	111
121	88	85	77	70	49	100	95

2. The following values represent the weekly point totals (in 48ths) for Ollie Mays for a 16-game season. Using graph paper, construct a stem-and-leaf plot and histogram based on the data below.

23	9	17	21	12	10	8	31
41	26	34	29	4	10	16	37

Statistics, data analysis, and probability

Name _____

Scatter Plots

1. The table below represents hypothetical ticket prices from 1990 to 1999. On graph paper, construct a scatter plot of these data. Does the scatter plot have a positive or negative correlation? Explain your answer.

Year	Average Price per Ticket
1990	$32.65
1991	$34.87
1992	$38.57
1993	$40.25
1994	$42.56
1995	$45.79
1996	$47.03
1997	$51.11
1998	$53.66
1999	$55.74

2. The table below shows the weight and maximum bench presses of several football players. Using graph paper, construct a scatter plot for these data. Does the scatter plot have a positive or negative correlation? Explain your answer.

Player	Weight of Player	Maximum Bench Press
A	225	320
B	190	250
C	345	450
D	330	425
E	255	410
F	255	430
G	340	480
H	330	490
I	185	260

Statistics, data analysis, and probability

Name _____

Box-and-Whisker Plots

The following data sets represent the weekly points earned (in 48ths) by Josh Maris and the total weekly team points earned by the Wildcats for the first twelve weeks of the season. Using graph paper, draw a box-and-whisker plot for each set of data. Label the medians as well as the upper and lower quartiles.

1. Josh Maris   23, 9, 17, 21, 12, 10, 8, 31, 37, 42, 35, 18

2. English Wildcats   66, 79, 38, 50, 106, 66, 69, 111, 49, 100, 95, 81

Statistics, data analysis, and probability   117

Name _____

Statements Using Math Terminology

Statements are complete sentences based on a set of data, and they must be accompanied by mathematical proof. The following statements were derived from week 1 on Handout 12.

Example

Ty Johnson earned one-fifth as many points as Jessie Wade earned.

$$\frac{1}{5} \times \frac{30}{48} = \frac{6}{48}$$

For the following statements, show the mathematical proof.

1. The wide receivers earned more points than the running backs did.

2. Jesse Wade and Ollie Mays accounted for over 63% of the total points earned by the Wildcats.

3. Angel Ramos earned approximately 8% of his team's total points.

4. D. J. Tucker earned twice as many points as the Tigers defense earned.

5. Josh Maris and Ty Johnson earned one-half as many points as D. J. Tucker earned.

6. Ollie Mays earned 27.4% of his team's total points.

7. Use Handout 12 to write five statements, and show the mathematical proof for each.
    1.
    2.
    3.
    4.
    5.

Mathematical reasoning

EXTRA CREDIT WORKSHEET

Extra Credit Problems

1. Each time a basketball bounces, it rebounds to 75% of its height on the previous rebound. The ball was originally dropped from the top of a building that has a height of 150 feet. Construct a table of the number of bounces and the rebound height of each bounce. On which bounce does the ball bounce less than 1 foot high?

2. Find the stadium seating capacity, average ticket price, and revenue for two professional football teams. In this case, revenue is defined as the number of tickets sold, multiplied by the average price of a ticket, multiplied by 8, which is the number of regular-season home games each team plays during one season.

   A. What is the difference in revenue between the two teams for one game? For one season?

   B. How much would revenue increase for one game for both teams if they increased ticket prices by an average of 5%?

   C. How much would revenue decrease for the season for both teams if they decreased ticket prices by an average of 3%?

3. Predict how many small (8-inch diameter), medium (12-inch diameter), or large (16-inch diameter) pizzas would fit on a football field. Then find the actual number of pizzas.

Assessment

Name _____

Pretest/Posttest

Show all of your work.

1. Find the sum of the points earned by the following players:

    Jesse Wade $\dfrac{36}{48}$ D. J. Tucker $\dfrac{2}{3}$

    Ty Johnson $\dfrac{5}{8}$ Tao Faumuina $\dfrac{5}{16}$

    Josh Maris $\dfrac{21}{48}$ Angel Ramos $\dfrac{1}{4}$

    Ollie Mays $\dfrac{1}{2}$ Tigers $\dfrac{1}{16}$

2. In problem 1, what is the ratio of the points earned by Mays to the points earned by Ramos?

3. In problem 1, convert Wade's points to a decimal and round to the nearest thousandth.

4. Evaluate

$$\frac{1}{8}\,(T) + \frac{1}{24}\,(V) + \frac{1}{48}\,(P + R + C) - \frac{1}{12}\,(I) - \frac{1}{16}\,(F)$$

    when
    $$T = 3$$
    $$V = 2$$
    $$P = 5$$
    $$R = 8$$
    $$C = 9$$
    $$I = 2$$
    $$F = 1$$

Pretest/Posttest *(Cont'd.)*

5. If one factor of $\frac{24}{48}$ is $\frac{4}{6}$, what is the second factor?

6. Write the prime factorization of 270, using exponential notation.

7. Convert $\frac{66}{48}$ into a mixed number, and write it in the simplest form.

8. Which is the greater rushing average per game: 1,225 yards in 9 games or 1,556 yards in 11 games?

9. If a player accumulated $2\frac{3}{8}$ points during the first 4 weeks of the season, how many points is he projected to earn for an entire 16-game season?

Pretest/Posttest *(Cont'd.)*

10. Based on the points earned by the players in problem 1 find the following:

    Range:

    Mean:

    Median:

    Mode:

11. Fill in the missing numbers in the patterns below:

    Donte Green $\qquad$ $\dfrac{1}{24}$ $\qquad$ $\dfrac{3}{48}$ $\qquad$ $\dfrac{1}{12}$ $\qquad$ _____

    Donny Taylor $\qquad$ $\dfrac{1}{16}$ $\qquad$ $\dfrac{1}{8}$ $\qquad$ $\dfrac{9}{48}$ $\qquad$ _____

12. The price of an autographed jersey rose from \$175 to \$345. Find the percentage of price increase.

13. If a player invests 55% of his annual salary of \$6.1 million at 8.5%, how much interest will he earn after one year?

14. A player has a practice field at his house. The dimensions of the field are 100 feet by 220 feet. Find the area of the field in square inches.

15. In problem 14, what is the length of the diagonal of the field?

Pretest/Posttest *(Cont'd.)*

16. The letters in "Lupe Crepp" are placed in a hat. Find the probability of the following random events:

    A. Selecting the letter p

    B. Selecting the letters p, u, or c

17. Solve for the variable in the following equation.

$$\frac{1}{8}(2) + \frac{1}{48}(P + 11 + 7) - \frac{1}{12}(2) - \frac{1}{16}(1) = \frac{37}{48}$$